Weird Combinations of Food Women Crave When Pregnant, and More ...

Written by Two Men

Weird Combinations of Food Women Crave When Pregnant, and More ...

Written by Two Men

A Complete Guide to Having a Baby

As presented by

Rafael Lujan and James Kelly

Published by Mammoth Star Publishing
www.mammothstarpublishing.com
www.authorjameskelly.com

Copyright © 2014
Registered Copyright © 2018

ISBN # 978-1-886726-36-9

LIBRARY OF CONGRESS CONTROL NUMBER: 2018954319

SAN: 256-5846

US $10.95

This book is interactive. If you have a smart phone with a barcode app, simply scan the QR code associated with each topic to see a video that further explains that subject.

Preface

Most of us have been around a pregnant woman at one time or another, whether it's our sister, friend, cousin or coworker. Even if we haven't been around a mother-to-be, we've all heard that women experience strange cravings while pregnant. Pickles and ice cream is the most common, but there are hosts of other strange food combinations that pregnant women crave, as well. This is not by accident. Women's bodies go through a series of hormonal changes throughout their pregnancy, and as a result, they begin to crave various nutrients needed to support themselves and their unborn child. Therefore, what the rest of us see as "weird combinations of food" may not be so weird after all.

In addition to looking at odd combinations of food, pregnant women eat and why, we will offer advice that any expectant mother can benefit from. Additionally, we will also look at what the father-to-be may be going through during the pregnancy, and the impact of having a child will have on both parents.

The idea for this book came about when a pregnant coworker dipped a slice of green apple in her salsa. Having two children of his own, Rafael Lujan began sharing his experience with pregnancy, and the concept for the book was born. James Kelly, being the avid fact finder, proceeded to research all the quirks and formalities of what new moms and dads go through. What started out as a humorous book on the weird cravings of pregnant women, soon turned into a "Pregnancy 101", covering everything from tips for optimal nutrition to fun facts like this one from babycenter.com. "The most popular day for babies to make their entrance is Tuesday, followed by Monday - Sunday is the slowest day. Scheduled C-sections and induced labors have a big influence on the fact that far fewer babies are born on the weekend, but spontaneous (non-scheduled) deliveries occur less often on the weekend too."

In compiling these facts, it was the authors' goal to inform new parents of what to expect, while providing a few laughs along the way.

Acknowledgements

We would like to thank those involved with the proofing and editing of this book.

Dana Micheli – A great editor and dear friend.

Stephen Murray – Author and friend who cares enough to review and make suggestions without asking. We truly appreciated his advice.

Norma Stewart -For taking the time out to review and advise.

Barry Goldberg – A great friend, who took the time to proofread and make numerous suggestions on this project.

Finally, to Rocio Mahoney – Already the mother of two beautiful girls (young women), and now in her ... (just realized we shouldn't say how old – women hate telling their age), she decided to have a third – a baby boy. It was the weird cravings she had during her son's pregnancy that inspired this book.

Table of Contents

Weird Combinations of Food Pregnant Women Eat

In researching this topic, we asked family, friends, acquaintances, and strangers about the unusual food combinations that they ate while pregnant or witnessed the pregnant women in their lives eating. After compiling these answers (and scouring the internet for more), we came up with the following list. It is by no means exhaustive.

1. Sauerkraut with a side of Easy Mac.
2. Rice with brown sugar, barbecue sauce.
3. Brownies with mustard or mac-n- cheese mixed with Lo Mein.
4. Pickles on Oreo cookies.
5. Tuna sandwiches with sea salt and malt vinegar potato chips.
6. Homemade vanilla ice cream on top of eggs
7. Scrambled eggs with cheese, ketchup and lots of horseradish sauce.
8. Combination pizza rolls dipped in white chocolate.

9. McDonald's chicken nuggets dipped in nacho cheese sauce.
10. Cheese pizza rolls dipped in vanilla pudding.
11. Sour Soothers candies dipped in cottage Cheese.
12. Miracle Whip mixed with grape jam and spread on saltine crackers.
13. Pickles on grilled cheese or peanut butter and jelly sandwiches.
14. Chocolate frosting on Ritz Crackers.
15. Black olives on cheesecake.
16. Bacon and banana sandwiches.
17. Chocolate chip cookies topped with chunky cottage cheese.
18. Chocolate cake with pinto beans.
19. Raw pasta dipped in peanut butter.
20. Bananas and apples smothered in tomato sauce.
21. Popcorn and chili sauce.
22. Bananas dipped in mayonnaise.
23. Peanut butter and tomato sandwiches.
24. Plain rice cakes with Laughing Cow cheese.
25. Sriracha sauce and a few fresh jalapenos.
26. Toasted English Muffin layered with peanut butter, cottage cheese and sliced bananas.
27. Mashed potatoes with ketchup.
28. Ketchup on corn.
29. Tuna sandwich with bacon and jalapenos.
30. Smoked salmon cream cheese and extra hot

horseradish sauce sandwiches.
31. French fries dipped in a chocolate sundae.
32. Egg and bacon over ice cream.
33. Caviar with white chocolate.
34. Creamy peanut butter on top of a hot hamburger, topped off with slices of white onion.
35. Baked bean and white bread sandwiches.
36. Strawberries and whipped cream and bacon.
37. Toast with a thin layer of butter, raspberry, or blackberry jam and topped with sliced cheese.
38. Peanut butter, mayonnaise and raw white onion.
39. Ketchup on pancakes.
40. Frito corn chips and caramel.
41. Bacon Twinkies.
42. Avocados on cinnamon toast.
43. Pepperoni and peanut butter sandwiches.
44. Hot Cheetos with pudding.
45. Ice cream with pepperonis.
46. Cabbage Rolls and chocolate milk.
47. Ice cream sandwich made with a hamburger bun.
48. Pineapple, banana, and cucumber pieces mixed together.
49. Cheeseburgers topped with jelly.
50. Chocolate chip cookies dipped in tomato salsa and ranch dressing.
51. Peanut butter, mayonnaise and sardines on

raisin bread.

52. Liverwurst and caramel.
53. Dill pickles, sardines, whipped cream, and chocolate ice cream – mixed all together.
54. Tuna and whipped cream sandwich
55. Mustard on a donut.
56. Ranch dressing on cake.
57. Anchovies on a peanut butter and jelly sandwich.
58. Peanut butter, bologna, and mayo sandwiches.
59. Tuna fish and plain yogurt.
60. Mustard on watermelon.
61. Hot sauce on Cheetos.
62. Pickles and peanut butter.
63. Peanut butter cookies and ketchup.
64. Bologna and maple syrup.
65. Cucumber, peanut butter and mayonnaise. sandwiches.
66. "Jezebel Sauce" -1 small can of black pepper, 1 jar horseradish, 1 jar apricot jelly. Mix then pour over 1 block of cream cheese. Spread on crackers.
67. Strawberry jam and salami on toast.
68. Peanut butter and horseradish on saltine crackers.
69. Mashed potatoes and macaroni-and-cheese mixed together.
70. Watermelon and feta.
71. Biscuits and gravy slathered in syrup.

72. Cottage cheese with pickled beets and mandarin oranges.
73. Peanut butter and jelly on sausage, egg-n-cheese English muffins.
74. Sauerkraut and mashed potatoes mixed together.
75. Sauerkraut added to a bowl of chili.
76. Triple-decker sandwich with mayo and bologna on the "bottom level" and peanut butter and banana on the second level.
77. Krispy Kreme donuts dipped in chocolate pudding.
78. Green apple slices dipped in salsa.
79. One of Lucy's favorite – Pistachio ice cream, topped with hot fudge and sardines.
80. Another of Lucy's favorite – a dill pickle dipped in a papaya juice milkshake.

Things You Should NEVER Say When Your Spouse is Pregnant

As you sit across the dinner table from your eight-months-pregnant wife and watch her devour half a roasted chicken like a Viking after a battle, NEVER say, "You must have been really hungry, there is nothing left but the bones." If you do, the daggers that will fly out of her eyes will be more piercing than any Viking's sword. In fact, do not even say, "How was it?" or "That must have been really good." Don't say anything! Just quietly get up, help your beautiful wife out of her chair, and escort her into the living room to watch television (making sure you take a bag of chips and a soda with you, or you will be making a return trip). Then go back into the kitchen and do the manly thing: clear the table and do the dishes, all without saying a word.

In the third trimester of her pregnancy, NEVER speak unless spoken to. Even saying the words "I love you" can be misconstrued. If you don't want to hear, "What does that mean? You're just saying that because I am fat, aren't you?", then keep your mouth shut. You'll be way ahead of the game.

When your wife wakes you at 2:00 a.m. and says she is craving something, NEVER say, "Okay, honey, just go back to sleep. I will pick some up on my way home after work." If it isn't in the house, I suggest you get up, get dressed, drive to the closest 24-hour market, and get whatever it is that she wants. Sure, you will lose one hour of sleep, but that doesn't compare to the guilt trip she will throw at you if you don't. Do you really want to hear, "You don't care about me and the baby" or "I'm carrying OUR child, so the least YOU could do is feed US when WE are hungry. Is that too much to ask?" Just do it, man!

When shopping with the mom-to-be for the baby's nursery, NEVER suggest what theme to use. Let her be the interior decorator. Your job is simple - drive the car, help your prego spouse in and out of the car, and open the doors to the twenty department stores you will undoubtedly be dragged into. You'll also be the on-call massage therapist, expected to rub her feet in-between stores, and the delivery man who runs down to the nearest eatery to get whatever it is she is craving while looking for the "perfect crib" (this, for a baby that won't even know how to say "crib" for two or three years). When have you ever heard of a child growing up to say, "You know that crib you guys put me in as a baby ... very uncomfortable! And that décor in my nursery ... what were you thinking?" Yeah, babies do that. They tend to remember everything.

NEVER assume that the house will be clean, the laundry will be done, and a meal will be on the table for the next nine months. Trust me on this. Just roll up your sleeves and take care of it.

NEVER tell your wife that she "just doesn't understand". No, *you* don't understand. Believe me, you will be opening a whole new can of worms with that comment, buddy!

NEVER tell your wife that, "this whole thing is hard for the both of us". Hmmm ... not a good idea. I'm thinking she probably won't agree. Who's carrying the baby?

NEVER ask your wife, "How are you feeling?" when she is having contractions. Duh!

When your wife asks if she looks fat, NEVER say "yes"; in fact, say "no" as fast as you can and without missing a beat. Come on, she is pregnant, not fat ... never fat.

When your wife starts randomly crying, just hold her ... if she lets you. NEVER try to fix the problem, there *is* no problem.

After a large meal, NEVER rub your stomach and say, "Oh man, I am so full I could pop!" Really, have you seen her belly?

NEVER indulge in or even discuss your own cravings ... just go with hers. It will be a lot simpler.

In the beginning of her pregnancy, NEVER tell your wife that she has been acting rather moody lately. Trust me, you haven't seen anything yet.

NEVER tell your wife you are feeling sick to your stomach and that you really don't feel like doing anything today. Think about it, she has probably thrown up three times before you put on your shoes that morning.

When coming in from a jog, NEVER feel offended if your wife doesn't want to snuggle. Again, think about it, she's more than likely feeling sweaty and dying of a hot flash. Why would she want to snuggle next to another hot and sweaty body?

NEVER thump on your spouse's stomach like it's a watermelon in order to make your child kick back. At least consider this before you do ... who really enjoys being punched and kicked over-and-over again?

NEVER mention that you want the baby here more than she does. When was the last time you carried *anything* around for nine months?

NEVER suggest to your wife that she have a natural childbirth ... especially if she is in her third trimester and a frying pan is within reach.

Finally - NEVER assume with any verbal exchange that you are right, whether during an argument or a regular conversation. For the next nine months, you will never be right ... if ever again.

Food Cravings
Foods Women Crave When Pregnant

As listed in the first chapter, it's pretty safe to say that unusual food cravings are quite common during pregnancy. In fact, more than sixty percent of pregnant women consistently crave one particular kind of food. Forty percent of them said they craved sweets, thirty-three percent craved salty snacks, and the remainder craved spicy food.

Most doctors and scientists believe that these cravings occur due to some nutritional deficiency in the mother's diet, and this is her body's way of telling her what she needs to eat.

Still, there is the debate: do these food cravings originate in the stomach or in the mind?

According to Nicole Cormier, RD, LDN, cravings can be caused by either physical or psychological needs. Emotional cravings or eating is triggered by psychological needs, whereas hunger is a biological function of the body's need for food. Emotional cravings can also lead to bingeing.

Most people, even those who are not pregnant, crave certain foods for various reasons. For example, when you have a bad day with the kids, you have to have cookies. If work does not go well, you rush to the vending machine for a candy bar. Some people crave popcorn whenever they watch a movie, while others drive by a donut shop and "have to have one".

Dr. John Foreyt, psychologist and director of the Nutrition Research Clinic at Baylor College of Medicine in Houston, helps people examine what causes their cravings. Most frequently, it is due to stress and tension.

Foreyt concedes that resisting these urges and cravings is one of the toughest challenges for weight-conscious people, especially when pregnant.

The majority of experts say there is a difference between real hunger and cravings. Hunger is a biological need to eat something because your stomach is empty. At this point, you are probably saying, "Well, duh!". However, what you may not know is that when most people are hungry they tend to prefer protein rather than high-sugar, high-fat foods. It is often the opposite with cravings.

Most obesity researchers contend that for many people, that the desire for certain foods is psychological; however, those same researchers are split as to whether a person's desire for food could possibly be biological.

Chocolate is one of the most commonly craved foods, for both men and women. This may be due to low blood sugar. The caffeine and sugar in chocolate raise your blood sugar levels. Dark chocolate is low on the glycemic index; therefore, it can even help stabilize blood sugar levels. Many people crave chocolate because their blood sugar levels have fallen and chocolate provides the sugar for quick energy. So keep in mind, if you find yourself feeling moody, irritable, shaky, and fatigued, especially between meals, then your chocolate cravings may be the result of low blood sugar levels.

For women, stress or changing hormonal levels prior to a woman's menstrual cycle can trigger a chocolate craving. Besides caffeine, fat, and sugar, chocolate also contains important trace minerals, like magnesium, which may be deficient in women prior to and during their menstrual cycles. Changing hormonal levels prior to and during the menstrual cycle can initiate all kinds of food cravings, and chocolate is one of them.

Nonetheless, there are researchers who claim that chocolate cravings in menstruating women may be a cultural phenomenon. Various studies have shown that American women are more likely to crave chocolate than women of other nationalities, which would seem to indicate that the craving is largely psychological. Let's face it, who the heck really knows? I say; if you crave it, eat it, so long as you don't overindulge.

Psychologist Kelly Brownell of Yale University suggests that when it comes to cravings, it is difficult to separate the psychological from the biological.

One thing for certain, cravings are hard to resist, especially for pregnant women. Fortunately, we don't always have to resist them. The research shows that people who do not allow themselves to give into cravings end up feeling deprived. In addition, these restrained eaters are the most likely to fall apart and binge. On the other hand, most cravings, when resisted, don't last for more than 10 minutes.

Pregnancy cravings differ from a regular craving in the sense that they are about a million times stronger. Pregnant women wake up craving a variety of foods and drinks, and they will often go out of their way to satisfy that craving (or force their partner to do so). Some have no shame in waking up their spouse in the middle of the night to go buy (and cook) bacon, stop by McDonald's for a burger, or DQ for ice cream. It's called, "What the baby wants, the baby gets!"

Here is one researchers results of the foods most pregnant women crave and why.

1. Ice
Pregnant women love to chew on ice. Yes, I know, ice is not really a food, but for some reason pregnant women just can't get enough of it. The reality is that many pregnant women who crave ice do it because it relieves inflammation of the mouth and tongue (a common symptom of anemia).

2. Chocolate
Chocolate (or other sweets) is something pregnant women can't seem to get enough of. This could be because chocolate makes you happy, and since pregnant women should not drink alcohol, chocolate is the next best thing. There is an old wives' tale that states, "If you crave sweets it means you're carrying a girl."

3. Spicy foods
Spicy foods, such as curry or hot red peppers, are often craved by pregnant women. This is because hot foods make the body sweat, which cools it off. If you are expecting and find it impossible to stay cool, try

adding some spice to your next meal. Surprisingly, it may help cool you down.

4. Pickles

Some people like the crunch, others like the vinegar; whatever the case, if you are craving pickles while pregnant, it may be because you are low in sodium. The good news is they are low in calories, easy to get and inexpensive.

5. Potato chips

Potato chips, like pickles, are loaded with salt, so, again, you could be low in sodium. However, more than likely you just desire something salty and crunchy. Keep in mind, potato chips are high in fat and calories, therefore you might want to try low-fat popcorn instead. It has been said that, "If she craves salty foods, she will have a boy".

6. Fruit

Many pregnant women crave fruit. This is a very good thing. Fruits, such as watermelons and grapes, are cool and refreshing, and provide your body, and your baby's, with vitamin C.

7. Lemon

It is well known that pregnant women crave sour foods. It is not unusual to see a pregnant women sucking on a lemon or adding it to her water. The reason is that the taste buds change during pregnancy and women often like to "shock" them with super-sour or super-spicy foods.

8. Ice cream
You will probably find women who are pregnant in the ice cream aisle more than any other in the supermarket. Ice cream is sweet and it cools down the body. Keep in mind, though, that weight is a concern, even during pregnancy. For a healthier option, think about buying low-fat frozen yogurt and top it off with fresh fruit. You may kill two cravings in one sitting.

9. Soda
A fizzy, carbonated soda may just be what you need for morning sickness. Carbonation settles the stomach, and may help to eliminate that queasy feeling you have been experiencing all day. Furthermore, try ginger ale or lemon-lime flavored sodas; caffeinated drinks should be avoided during pregnancy.

10. Coffee
Even though coffee is commonly craved by pregnant women, doctors say you should avoid it, especially if you drank it before conceiving. On the other hand, coffee makes you more alert and decreases headaches and depression. Caution: always check with your doctor before deciding to partake in a soothing cup of Joe.

There are numerous surveys on the Internet about the foods pregnant women crave. Here are the results of another "top ten".

1. Watermelon
2. Pickles
3. Chocolate cream-filled Twinkies
4. Brussels sprouts with scrambled eggs
5. Munchos and salty chips
6. Cheeseburgers
7. Pistachio ice cream
8. Gingersnap cookies
9. Pancakes with maple syrup
10. Coffee grounds (I know this sounds weird, but I like them too!)

The Contenders

11. Oranges
12. Nachos
13. Pizza

A third survey, from shareranks.com, lists the following:

1. Pickles
2. Peanut Butter
3. Cheese
4. Cherries
5. Green Olives
6. Chocolate

7. Bacon
8. Steak
9. Milk
10. Ice Cream

The Contenders
11. Watermelon
12. Peaches
13. Chips
14. Sweets

Yet another survey suggests the following:
1. Chocolate
2. Pickles
3. Eggs - They are a fantastic source of protein.
4. Cheese - This is perhaps due to the body's need for calcium. However, too much of it can lead to extra weight gain. An alternative would be calcium-rich veggies like leafy greens and broccoli.
5. Bacon
6. Lemons
7. Ice Cream
8. Fruit
9. Chili Peppers
10. Peanut Butter

What an Expectant Mother Should Be Eating

To ensure a healthy pregnancy, the diet of a mother-to-be needs to be balanced and nutritious. Her diet should include the right balance of proteins, carbohydrates and fats, and a wide variety of vegetables and fruits. In order for the baby to develop and grow properly, the woman will want to make certain that her diet provides enough nutrients and energy for both her and the baby. After all, eating right is the best way to make sure that the expectant mom's body is healthy enough to deal with the changes that will take place.

Without a doubt, a pregnant woman's calorie intake will grow during her pregnancy. Contrary to popular belief, however, this does not mean that she should literally "eat for two"; her calorie consumption does not double, it just goes up. According to the Institute of Medicine, USA, weight gain recommendations may also vary, depending on the woman's age, fetal development, and her current health. Consult your obstetrician to find out what the best diet is for you. Just keep in mind: up to the eighth week of pregnancy, the baby is considered an "embryo". Therefore, calorie intake may not be as significant. After that, once its major structures have formed, it is considered a fetus and may require a higher caloric intake. As a rule of thumb, a woman who is not overweight at the start of her pregnancy should gain between 25 to 35 pounds by the end of the nine months.

A mother-to-be should follow a nutritious and balanced diet that includes:

1. Fruits and Vegetables – You should eat five portions of fruits and/or vegetables every day. Most experts believe that eating fruit and vegetables is better for you than just drinking the juice.

2. Carbohydrate-rich foods – This will include potatoes, rice, pasta, and bread.

3. Proteins – This includes fish, lean meat and chicken, as well as eggs. If you are a vegan, consider the following foods as good sources of protein: Quinoa (known as a "complete protein", with all the essential amino acids), tofu and soy products. Beans, lentils, legumes (all three are also rich in iron), and nut butters.

British and Brazilian researchers reported in the journal *PLoS ONE* (July 2013 issue) that pregnant women who regularly ate seafood had lower levels of anxiety compared to their counterparts who did not. Pregnant mothers who never consumed seafood had a

53% greater risk of suffering from high levels of anxiety, the authors wrote.

4. Fats – Fat should not make up more than 30% of a pregnant woman's daily caloric intake. Researchers from the University of Illinois reported in the *Journal of Physiology* that a high-fat diet might genetically program the baby for future diabetes.

Team leader Professor Yuan-Xiang Pan said, "We found that exposure to a high-fat diet before birth modifies gene expression in the livers of offspring so they are more likely to overproduce glucose, which can cause early insulin resistance and diabetes."

5. Fiber - Wholegrain foods, such as wholegrain bread, wild rice, wholegrain pasta, pulses, fruit, and vegetables are all rich in fiber. Research shows that pregnant women have a higher risk of developing constipation. Therefore, eating plenty of fiber is effective in minimizing that risk. Studies have also shown that eating plenty of fiber during a pregnancy can reduce the risk of hemorrhoids. In addition, the right amount of fiber in your diet can help prevent excessive weight gain.

6. Calcium - It is important that the mother-to-be maintain a healthy intake of calcium. Dairy

foods, such as milk, cheese, and yoghurt are rich in calcium. If the mother-to-be is vegan, she should consider calcium-fortified soymilk and juices, calcium-set tofu, soybeans, bok choy, broccoli, collard greens, Chinese cabbage, okra, mustard greens, kale, and soy nuts.

7. Zinc – This vital trace element plays a major role in normal growth and development, cellular integrity and several biological functions, including nucleic acid metabolism and protein synthesis. Since all these functions are involved in growth and cell division, zinc is important for the growth and development of the fetus.

Chicken, turkey, ham, shrimp, crabs, oysters, meat, fish, dairy products, beans, peanut butter, nuts, sunflower seeds, ginger, onions, bran, wheat germ, rice, pasta, cereals, eggs, lentils, and tofu are your best sources of zinc.

8. Iron – Iron makes up a major part of your hemoglobin, the oxygen-carrying pigment, and main protein in the red blood cells. Iron also assists in the delivery of oxygen to the muscles so that they can function properly, and it

increases the resistance to stress and disease.

The following foods are a rich source of iron:

Dried beans, dried fruits (such as apricots), egg yolks, some cereals (if they are fortified with iron), liver (*note: liver is rich in iron, but doctors and most nutritionists advise pregnant women to avoid liver because it is also very high in vitamin A. Excessive amounts of vitamin A may harm the baby during pregnancy*), lean meats, oysters (just make sure they are cooked if you are pregnant), poultry, salmon, tuna, lamb, pork, shellfish, legumes (lima beans, soybeans, kidney beans, dried beans and peas), seeds (Brazil nuts and almonds), vegetables (especially dark green ones like broccoli, spinach, dandelion leaves, asparagus, collards, and kale), and whole grains (brown rice, oats, millet, and wheat).

Should I Take Supplements?

(Always consult your doctor first)

Do I Need Extra Iron?

The answer is probably yes. As mentioned above, iron is critical to our body's oxygen delivery system and helps fight off disease. After all, when pregnant, a woman's body absorbs iron more efficiently.

Additionally, a pregnant woman should consume more of it in order to make sure that both she and her baby have an adequate oxygen supply. Keep in mind that during pregnancy, the amount of blood in a woman's body increases by almost 50%. Therefore, she will need an increase of iron to make more hemoglobin for all that extra blood, as well as for the growing placenta and the developing baby. An added benefit of maintaining a healthy level of iron during pregnancy is that it can help prevent depression, weakness, tiredness, and irritability.

Studies have shown that most women start their pregnancy without an adequate amount of iron to meet the increasing demands of their bodies, particularly after the third or fourth month. It is important to note that if the iron stores are inadequate the mother may become anemic.

According to the United Nations, approximately 47% of non-pregnant females and 60% of pregnant females have anemia globally. If iron-deficient women without anemia are included, the figure is 60% of non-pregnant and 90% of pregnant women. In rich nations, approximately 18% of non-pregnant and 30% of pregnant women are iron-deficient; however, those figures are higher among those with lower incomes.

What are the risks of iron deficiency during a pregnancy?

1. Preterm delivery - the baby is born early; a premature baby
2. Low birth weight
3. Stillbirth - the baby dies before it is delivered
4. Newborn death - the baby dies soon after it is born
5. Tiredness, irritability, depression (in the mother) during the pregnancy

Also, consider this: if the mother-to-be is anemic later in the pregnancy, there is a higher risk of losing a lot of blood when she gives birth.

You should understand that the human body less easily absorbs non-animal sources of iron, even when those sources are high in iron. Mixing some lean meat, fish, or poultry with them can improve their absorption rate by up to three times.

You should also note that some teas, such as commercial black tea or pekoe teas, have chemicals that bind to iron and make it much harder for the body to absorb.

What about Folic Acid?

The National Health Service (NHS), UK, recommends that a pregnant woman use supplements such as folic acid (400 micrograms) per day up to the 12th week of pregnancy. Ideally, women should have been on them before becoming pregnant.

The human body does not store folic acid, so we should consume it every day in order to maintain adequate amounts. According to the British Dietetic Association, vitamin B9 (folic acid and folate inclusive) is vital for several bodily functions, including the aid of rapid cell division and growth, and the production of healthy red blood cells. Vitamin B9 also helps synthesize and repair DNA and RNA. Folic acid enhances brain health, and Dutch researchers have reported that it may improve memory. It is especially important for pregnant women to supplement folic acid in their diet in order to prevent major birth defects of their baby's brain or spine, including neural tube defects such as spina bifida and anencephaly.

The types of food that contain folic acid are asparagus, baker's yeast, broccoli, Brussels sprouts, cabbage, cauliflower, egg yolk, jacket potato (large), kidney beans, black beans, lentils, lettuce, milk, oranges, parsnips, peas, spinach, sunflower seeds, and whole-wheat bread (usually fortified). Many fruits have moderate amounts of folic acid; papaya and kiwi have more.

The majority of women can get adequate amounts of most nutrients if they follow a healthy diet. However, some may need supplements to prevent a deficiency. Always consult your doctor about taking any supplement.

Are Vitamin D Supplements Good for Me?

Some guidelines suggest that a pregnant woman take supplements containing 10 mcg of vitamin D daily. Summer sunlight is a good source of vitamin D (the light does not have the vitamin but triggers the skin to synthesize it). Furthermore, exposure to sunlight should be limited, because too much can cause sunburn and raise the risk of developing skin cancer.

Should You Take Zinc During Pregnancy?

Zinc deficiency during pregnancy may adversely affect both mother and fetus. One observational study published in the Food and Nutrition Bulletin reported that pregnant women on zinc supplements were 14% less likely to have a premature delivery.

Supplements to Avoid

Unless your doctor tells you otherwise, you should avoid vitamin A supplements - this includes high dose multivitamins. Pregnant women should avoid taking too much vitamin A, as this may harm the baby. You should also avoid cod liver oil supplements, again, unless your doctor tells you otherwise.

Foods and Things to Avoid During a Pregnancy

Avoid soft mold-ripened cheese, such as blue-veined cheese, Brie or Camembert, as they may increase the risk of Listeria infection (listeriosis). Listeria is a group of bacteria that can cause potentially fatal infections to pregnant women and their babies.

You should avoid any type of pâté, whether vegetable or meat-based. The risk here is also of Listeria infection.

Always avoid uncooked or undercooked ready-prepared meals during your pregnancy. It is crucial that prepackaged meals are cooked thoroughly until they are piping hot. The risk of listeriosis, as well as infection from other pathogens, is a concern.

Never eat raw eggs, including any foods with raw or partially cooked eggs in them. Eggs should be cooked well in order to avoid the risk of salmonellosis (salmonella infection).

You should always avoid undercooked or partially cooked meat.
When gardening, make sure to wear gloves and wash your hands afterwards. Toxoplasmosis, a parasite that

lives in soil, can cause an infection that can harm the unborn baby. Cat feces may also harbor this parasite; so, use gloves when cleaning the cat litter box.

Always cook shellfish thoroughly. A risk of bacterial or viral contamination, which can cause food poisoning, is the biggest concern.

In certain types of fish, be cautious of mercury. Shark, swordfish, and marlin should be avoided, or at the very least kept to a minimum. Many experts believe that tuna should be limited to one serving per week.

Foods that are high in sugar and fat should be kept to a minimum, such as cakes, biscuits, cookies, and candy. They have very little nutritional content, and may undermine a pregnant woman's efforts at maintaining a healthy body weight.

Should Pregnant Women Drink Alcohol?

It is vital that you understand that when a woman consumes alcohol, it passes from her blood, through the placenta and to the baby. A fetus' liver is one of the last organs to develop. The fetus does not fully mature until well into the second half of pregnancy. Therefore, a fetus' liver cannot process alcohol as well as an adult's. The concern should be that too much exposure to alcohol might seriously undermine the baby's development. Understandably, most healthcare professionals advise pregnant women to avoid alcohol altogether.

With alcohol consumption, there is an increased risk that the baby will develop FAS (fetal alcohol syndrome), which may stunt growth and cause behavioral disorders later on, as well as learning problems. In addition, there is the risk of facial abnormalities.

Should Pregnant Women Avoid Caffeine?
Unfortunately for the mom-to-be, consuming too much caffeine during pregnancy may increase the risk of low birth weight. When a child is born underweight, it can lead to health problems. There is also a higher risk of miscarriage.

While we often associate caffeine and coffee, it is important to remember that many other foods and drinks such as sodas, energy drinks, chocolate, and tea are also caffeinated. In addition, pregnant women should always consult a doctor or pharmacist before taking a cold or flu remedy, as a number of these medications contain caffeine as well.

Despite the concerns, most health authorities around the world say that coffee does not need to be cut out completely. However, it should not exceed more than 200 mg per day, or two cups.

Proper Weight

A common problem for pregnant women is figuring out how to eat healthy without gaining too much weight. According to Elizabeth Ward, MS, RD, a freelance writer and nutrition consultant, if a woman has a lot of excess body fat at the time of conception, there is an increased risk of neural tube defects such as spina bifida. A developmental congenital disorder caused by the incomplete closing of the embryonic neural tube, spina bifida comes with a host of physical problems, including leg weakness and paralysis, orthopedic abnormalities (i.e., club foot, hip dislocation, scoliosis), bladder and bowel control problems (i.e., incontinence, urinary tract infections, and poor renal function), pressure sores, skin irritations, and abnormal eye movement. Neural tube defects can usually be detected during a pregnancy by testing the mother's blood (AFP screening) or by a detailed fetal ultrasound.

Given the above, it is as important for women to maintain a normal body weight before and during a pregnancy. It gives the child a better chance of developing normally, and lowers the risk of several complications during pregnancy, including high blood pressure and gestational diabetes. An overweight mother is also at risk of delivering a baby that is too large, sometimes necessitating a Cesarean section.

We used to think of pregnancy as a sedentary time; however, we now know that reasonable exercise is not just permissible, but important for a healthy pregnancy. Exercise can help maintain proper weight control, keep blood pressure in check, and improve circulation and strength. It also reduces stress and may even help you sleep better. Never start an exercise routine or diet without contacting your doctor first.

What is Pica?

As discussed earlier, food cravings during pregnancy are completely normal. However, if an expectant mother is troubled by *what* she is craving, she may have a condition known as Pica (pronounced *pie-kah*).

Pica is an eating disorder that mostly affects women and children. Someone with Pica will crave non-food items, such as ice, plaster, cigarette butts, and other harmful items.

This condition has been linked to dietary deficiencies; however, there are many factors that can cause a person to develop Pica. If you suspect that you have Pica, inform your doctor immediately, as consuming non-food items can be deadly. In many cases, once the dietary deficiencies are corrected, the cravings decrease significantly.

It's Called COUVADE
When Men Get Cravings
Just Like Mom

The father-to-be can also experience weird food cravings, morning sickness, and even a swollen belly during his partner's pregnancy.

Dr. Arthur Brennan of London's Kingston University studied 282 fathers-to-be and found that 55% of them were experiencing symptoms that most of us associate with pregnant women. He believes this was caused by elevated levels of prolactin, a hormone normally associated with breast-feeding mothers. Prolactin was also present in the expectant fathers in Brennan's study.

There have also been instances of fathers-to-be suffering cramps, mood swings, food cravings, and morning sickness. In extreme cases, their symptoms may include labor pains, postpartum depression, and even nosebleeds. Perhaps this is nature's way of preparing the men for fatherhood. Tests have shown that fathers-to-be experience hormonal changes (including a drop in testosterone) during their partner's pregnancy that brings out their gentler, more nurturing side. Now you can understand why even the most macho of men cry at the birth of their child.

According to Wikipedia

Also known as "sympathetic pregnancy", the term couvade (pronounced "kü-väd" or "koo-vahd") was coined by anthropologist E. B. Tylor in 1865 to refer to certain rituals fathers across several cultures adopt during pregnancy.

The word itself is derived from the French verb *"couver"*, which means "to brood or hatch". The modern use of the word is a misunderstanding of an earlier idiom *"faire la couvade"*, which means, "to sit doing nothing."

For example, the Cantabri people (a pre-Roman Celtic people and large tribal federation) enacted a custom in which the father, during or immediately after the birth of a child, would take to bed and complain of having labor pains. In Papua New Guinea, one tradition was for the father-to-be to build a hut outside the village and mimic the mother's labor pains until the baby was born. Similar rituals have be found in other cultural groups throughout Thailand, Russia, China, and even several indigenous groups in the Americas.

Some cultures believe sympathetic pregnancy is attributed to efforts to ward off demons or spirits from the mother, or perhaps to seek favor of supernatural beings for their child.

Couvade is not a new concept in the scientific world. Throughout history, travelers have reported such incidents, including the Greek geographer Strabo and the Venetian traveler Marco Polo.

Symptoms of couvade include variations in appetite, weight gain, nausea, insomnia, indigestion, diarrhea/constipation, headaches, toothaches, mood swings, backache, itchy skin, and of course, food cravings.

Most symptoms occur during the third and fourth months, and then reoccur as the birth approaches. The good news for the father-to-be is that all symptoms disappear after the child is born.

Whether psychological or a strange biological occurrence, one thing is for sure, couvade is a reality that some fathers will have to contend with.

The Financial Reality of Having a Child

During this joyous time, the last thing expectant parents should have to worry about is money; yet, for many men and women, it tops the list of concerns. This is not surprising, given that having a child is an enormous financial undertaking.

Statistics show that raising a child to the age of 18 can cost upwards of $100,000 to over $500,000! The child's first year alone may set you back $10,000.

Of course, planning a child is the best way to ensure the finances will be there; however, according to the Alan Guttmacher Institute in New York, up to 49% of the pregnancies in the U.S. are unplanned. This includes pregnancies happening both inside marriage (or committed relationships) and those happening to single women.

The best advice, before or immediately after the child is born, is to start a separate savings account for that child. Set aside a determined percentage of your net income (minimum of 5 %), and diligently tuck it away. By starting early, you will be amazed at how much it will grow over time. Once your child is in their teenage years, that account will undoubtedly come in handy - especially if that child decides to go off to college.

The Baby Shower

A baby shower is a tradition that goes back to ancient times, with a twofold purpose: it was a chance for friends, family, and neighbors to stop by and wish the expectant mother well, and also to pass along baby items their own children no longer needed.

Baby showers were historically given only for the family's first child, and only women were invited. It was a way for women to share wisdom and lessons on the art of becoming a mother. As the tradition grew, baby showers were held when the mom-to-be was at least seven or eight months pregnant, and were hosted by a close friend. This was because it was considered rude for families to beg for gifts on behalf of another family member. However, this custom has changed, and today it varies by culture and region. In some regions of the world, a close female family member— usually the baby's grandmother hosts the baby shower.

In modern times, these events have expanded to include mothers of adopted children or to include men on the guest list. Some expectant mothers wind up having more than one baby shower (i.e., one with friends and another with co-workers).

Today, there are no set rules for where or when to hold a baby shower. The host usually determines the guests and style of entertainment—usually baby-themed games and activities. There is always food, but not a full meal.

As mentioned earlier, baby showers will vary across cultures. For example, Mexican baby showers are usually on a much larger scale than American baby showers - more people, more food, and more partying! Friends and family are invited, including men. There is usually a full meal, not just snacks or finger food. Moreover, like most Latino celebrations, this joyous occasion lasts late into the night.

Gifts

Guests should bring small gifts to the shower –things like diapers, blankets, baby bottles, clothes, and toys that the mother will need once the baby arrives. It is common to open the gifts during the party.

International

Baby showers are popular all around the world. Here are a few examples.

1. In Canada, it is still a "women only" event.
2. In Brazil, a party called "chá de bebê" (baby tea) is offered before birth and is attended only by women.
3. In China, a baby shower, called *manyue*, is held one month after the baby is born. Both family and friends celebrate this tradition.

4. In Armenia, a baby shower is called "qarasunq" (քառասունք) and is held 40 days after the baby's birth. Again, both family and friends celebrate. Guests usually bring gifts for the baby or parents.

5. In Iran, a baby shower is called a sismoony party. One to three months before the child is born, the family and close friends will provide the mother with virtually everything she needs for her first baby, including a bed, toys, clothes, and dishes.

6. In Costa Rica, a baby shower party is called a *té de canastilla* ("basket tea").

7. A traditional Islamic event around the birth of a baby is called "Aqiqah". Animals are sacrificed and the meat is then divided in three equal parts; one part is for the poor and needy, one is for relatives and friends, which can involve inviting them at home for a feast, and finally, the last part of the slaughtered animal is for the household.

8. In South Africa, a baby shower is called a stork party. It is usually a "surprise" party, which takes place when the mother is about six months pregnant. Traditionally, men were not invited, but traditions have changed. Dressings up, as well as the giving of necessary baby supplies accompany the stork party.

9. Only women attend a baby shower in Guatemala. It is not unusual for middle class women to have more than one baby shower (one with close friends, co-workers, family, etc.).

The Top Ten Baby Shower Themes

1. Playroom Theme
The playroom theme is perhaps one of the best themes for a baby shower party. The decorations, as well as the accents, will remind you and the guests of the joys of childhood.

2. Sports Theme
Various themes can be used such as baseball, basketball, football, soccer, auto racing, gymnastics, swimming, etc.

3. Summer Fun
The Fun under the Sun - Take your love of the beach and recreate it for your baby shower party.

4. Christmas Theme
St. Nick waving - Are you expecting your little bundle of joy to be delivered by the stork during the holidays? A Christmas-themed baby shower will definitely give the yuletide season a new meaning.

5. Jungle Safari Theme
A Jaguar in the jungle - The jungle safari is a cute and wonderful theme for your baby shower.

6. Space Theme

Planets - Mobiles of the various planets can be hung from the ceiling, or used as centerpieces on the tables. Pictures of various Constellations can be taped to the wall. Toy spaceships or rockets can also be used as centerpieces or also hung from the ceiling. Who knows, your child might be the next Neil Armstrong!

7. Flower Theme

An owl surrounded by Buttercups - If you are expecting your little baby to arrive in the early days of spring, then the flower theme is just right for your party.

8. Under the Sea

Ariel of "The Little Mermaid" - Now you can make your childhood dream to be a mermaid come true by throwing an under-the-sea theme party for your baby shower.

9. Cowboy

Cowboys of Texas - Rodeos, horses, sheriffs, and cowboys! This theme is fun and ideal if you are expecting a baby boy.

10. Princess Theme

Princess Pech of Mario Brothers or Cinderella - A baby girl in the family deserves to be treated like a princess. If you are expecting a baby girl, then this theme is perfect for you.

Seven Traditional Baby Shower Games

Baby Shower Bingo

Like regular bingo, Baby Shower Bingo is played by marking squares on a card until the first person fills in an entire line and wins.

You can buy preprinted bingo cards, find free ones online that provide an alternative way to play, or make your own. The numbers on the cards should not be greater than the number of presents.

First, number each present brought to the shower (based on the number of presents). Alternatively, you can have pictures of baby items on the cards, such as a teddy bear, books, or bibs. As the guest of honor opens each present randomly, have her call out the number of that present. Then have each guest mark the number called out on their bingo card. Bingo is achieved once a row is completed up and down, across or corner to corner on the card. The first player to achieve a vertical, horizontal, or diagonal line wins.

The Clothes Pin Game

Don't Say Baby! - The idea is to avoid the word "baby" throughout the shower. This is played by giving several colored clothespins to each guest. Each time someone slips and says, "baby", the person who catches the slip-up gets to take the offender's clothespin. The person who has acquired the most pins at the end of the shower wins.

How big is Mommy?

The idea of this game is to guess how big the expectant mom's tummy is at the time of the shower. Pass around spools of ribbon, balls of string or yarn to each guest, along with a pair of scissors. Each guest will try to estimate how big around the mother-to-be's belly, and then clip off a piece of ribbon, string or yarn to fit that size. After each guest has cut their piece of string, they will then take turns placing it around the new mom's belly - The one who guesses the closest wins.

Scramble Words

Make a list of 15 or 20 different terms, such as blanket, pacifier, bassinet, diaper, or stroller. Then scramble the letters of each word; example, "tlarte" for rattle. At the shower, give each guest a piece of paper with the scrambled words on, or you can post the words on a wall or chalkboard where everyone can view them at the same time. Set a timer for two or more minutes. Whoever solves the most scrambled words in that time wins the game.

Team Diaper Duty

To play "Team Diaper Duty", pair the guests into teams of two. Each team will go one at a time. Time each team with a stopwatch as they try to remove the clothes from a doll, take off the diaper, and put the new diaper on as neatly as it would be for a real baby, then put the clothes back on. Once the doll is completely dressed again, stop the watch. To make it fun, each team member can only use one hand! The fastest team wins.

Who's that Baby?

This picture game is an excellent icebreaker for showers where not all the guests might know each other.

With the baby shower invitations, include a request that each guest bring one of their own baby pictures. Then, at the shower, hang all the photos where everyone can see them, or place them on a table. Then number the pictures, and hand out a piece of paper and pen. Have each guest write down the number associated with the picture, look at each guest in the room, and write down who they think the baby in that picture is. You can time this event for say, about 15 minutes, or you can allow guests to keep making their matches throughout the shower until the end. The person with the most correct guesses wins.

Baby Face

This game can be very funny - In this game, the host must find photos of the expectant mom and dad, as well as their siblings. Before the shower, make several copies of the photos, and then cut out the eyes, noses, mouths, ears, hair or any other facial features. Next, create an outline of a baby's head on a piece of paper. Make a copy of that outline for each guest.

To play, place the cutouts in a pile and have each guest select different facial features from that pile, and then glue them onto their copy of the outline. The idea is to have each guest create a representation of what they think the baby will look like.

Awards
Prizes for all the games can be gift cards, candy (i.e. boxes of gourmet chocolates), toiletries, lotions, soaps, or perfumes.

Baby Showers for Fathers

In today's society, baby showers can also be given for the father-to-be; they are usually quite a bit different from that of the expectant mother. These so-called "diaper parties" often include drinking beer, watching sports, fishing, or playing video games. As you may have guessed, the primary gifts are diapers and/or diaper-related items. The organizer of the diaper party is typically a friend of the father-to-be. Whereas a mother-to-be may have a baby shower at home, a father-to-be may have their shower held at a local bar, a friend's house, or the soon-to-be grandfather's house.

In the United Kingdom, a baby shower for a father-to-be is called *wetting the baby's head*, and is seen more commonly than baby showers, which are viewed as a materialistic U.S. custom. *Wetting the baby's head* is traditionally when the father celebrates the birth by having a few drinks with a group of friends.

Baby Names

Top Unusual Boy Names

1. Asher - Hebrew for "happy" or "blessing"
2. Stelios - Greek for "pillar, Orthodox saint, protector of children"
3. Kaden - Irish (variation of Cayden) for "fighter", with two other meanings in different countries and cultures
4. Garret - English for "to watch", "rules by the spear", or "hard/bold spear"
5. Uri - Hebrew for "My light" or "My fire"
6. Guillermo - Spanish version of the name "William"

Top Unusual Girl Names

1. Raya - Israeli for "friend"
2. Danika - Russian for "morning star"
3. Teagan - Irish for "Attractive, Little poet"
4. Elspeth - Hebrew Name - Variant of Elisabeth: From Elisheba, meaning either "oath of God" or "God is satisfaction"
5. Diamond - Latin *diamas,* from Latin *adamas*, Greek origin meaning "invincible, untamed"
6. Sidra - Israeli for "Star Born; of the stars"

Top Baby Names for 2017 According to the Social Security Administration

(Statistics come out in August of each year for the pior year .)

History

In 1998, the Social Security Administration published Actuarial Note #139, Name Distributions in the Social Security Area, August 1997, on the distribution of given names of Social Security number holders.

Data Source

All names are from Social Security card applications for births that occurred in the United States after 1879. Note that many people born before 1937 never applied for a Social Security card, so their names are not included in our data. For others who did apply, the SSA records may not show the place of birth, and again their names are not included in their data.

Names that increased in popularity from 2016 to 2017

Male			
Name	**Increase**	**2016**	**2017**
Wells	504	915	1419
Kairo	423	803	1226
Caspian	328	868	1196
Nova	323	918	1241
Colson	323	736	1059
Kace	315	870	1185
Kashton	302	641	943
Koa	294	939	1233
Gatlin	282	957	1239
Bjorn	276	953	1229

Female			
Name	**Increase**	**2016**	**2017**
Ensley	1461	965	2426
Oaklynn	1072	886	1958
Dream	840	828	1668
Oaklyn	749	676	1425
Melania	720	930	1650
Emberly	616	629	1245
Octavia	435	593	1028
Paisleigh	364	840	1204
Yara	352	987	1339
Kehlani	347	522	869

Top 5 Baby Names By State
(For births in 2017)

Alabama				
Rank	Male name	Number of males	Female name	Number of females
1	William	398	Ava	358
2	James	315	Olivia	300
3	Elijah	303	Emma	240
4	John	297	Harper	192
5	Noah	252	Amelia	190

Alaska				
Rank	Male name	Number of males	Female name	Number of females
1	James	47	Emma	56
2	Liam	45	Olivia	56
3	Wyatt	40	Aurora	38
4	William	38	Isabella	38
5	Noah	37	Sophia	35

Arizona				
Rank	Male name	Number of males	Female name	Number of females
1	Liam	404	Emma	446
2	Noah	380	Isabella	400
3	Sebastian	344	Olivia	394
4	Alexander	329	Mia	380
5	Julian	298	Sophia	374

Arkansas				
Rank	Male name	Number of males	Female name	Number of females
1	Elijah	170	Emma	176
2	William	146	Olivia	155
3	Noah	142	Ava	150
4	Liam	133	Harper	138
5	Mason	125	Isabella	108

California				
Rank	Male name	Number of males	Female name	Number of females
1	Noah	2,511	Emma	2,726
2	Sebastian	2,264	Mia	2,588
3	Liam	2,180	Olivia	2,474
4	Ethan	2,141	Sophia	2,430
5	Matthew	2,120	Isabella	2,337

Colorado				
Rank	Male name	Number of males	Female name	Number of females
1	Liam	315	Emma	292
2	Oliver	297	Olivia	271
3	William	268	Charlotte	257
4	Noah	267	Evelyn	252
5	Benjamin	253	Isabella	246

Connecticut				
Rank	Male name	Number of males	Female name	Number of females
1	Noah	222	Olivia	230
2	Liam	208	Emma	219
3	Logan	189	Ava	169
4	Jacob	187	Mia	162
5	Michael	175	Sophia	159

Delaware				
Rank	Male name	Number of males	Female name	Number of females
1	Logan	56	Olivia	56
2	Noah	55	Ava	55
3	Liam	53	Charlotte	49
4	Mason	52	Isabella	45
5	Michael	49	Emma	44

District of Columbia				
Rank	Male name	Number of males	Female name	Number of females
1	James	93	Ava	56
2	Henry	83	Olivia	52
3	William	80	Eleanor	51
4	Noah	76	Genesis	41
5	Jacob	59	Elizabeth	39

Florida				
Rank	Male name	Number of males	Female name	Number of females
1	Liam	1,352	Isabella	1,306
2	Noah	1,275	Emma	1,241
3	Lucas	1,030	Olivia	1,168
4	Elijah	938	Sophia	1,057
5	Matthew	910	Ava	1,019

Georgia				
Rank	Male name	Number of males	Female name	Number of females
1	William	685	Ava	667
2	Noah	609	Olivia	569
3	Mason	543	Emma	531
4	Elijah	522	Isabella	460
5	James	509	Charlotte	391

Hawaii				
Rank	Male name	Number of males	Female name	Number of females
1	Liam	78	Emma	73
2	Noah	64	Olivia	64
3	Mason	60	Aria	51
4	Elijah	56	Ava	47
5	Logan	55	Chloe	46

Idaho				
Rank	Male name	Number of males	Female name	Number of females
1	Oliver	115	Emma	105
2	Liam	99	Olivia	96
3	William	93	Charlotte	89
4	James	83	Evelyn	88
5	Mason	81	Harper	76

Illinois				
Rank	Male name	Number of males	Female name	Number of females
1	Noah	769	Olivia	726
2	Liam	662	Emma	701
3	Benjamin	621	Ava	615
4	Logan	596	Sophia	598
5	Alexander	583	Isabella	583

Indiana

Rank	Male name	Number of males	Female name	Number of females
1	Oliver	386	Emma	448
2	Liam	384	Olivia	391
3	Elijah	343	Amelia	352
4	Noah	337	Charlotte	342
5	William	335	Harper	333

Iowa

Rank	Male name	Number of males	Female name	Number of females
1	Oliver	210	Harper	173
2	Liam	180	Emma	170
3	Henry	179	Olivia	166
4	Lincoln	158	Charlotte	160
5	Wyatt	153	Evelyn	155

Kansas				
Rank	Male name	Number of males	Female name	Number of females
1	Oliver	170	Emma	202
2	William	160	Olivia	182
3	Liam	150	Ava	154
4	Jackson	140	Harper	151
5	Henry	139	Evelyn	144

Kentucky				
Rank	Male name	Number of males	Female name	Number of females
1	William	302	Emma	290
2	Elijah	283	Ava	243
3	Noah	275	Olivia	236
4	Liam	265	Harper	235
5	James	256	Isabella	210

Louisiana				
Rank	Male name	Number of males	Female name	Number of females
1	Liam	253	Olivia	296
2	Noah	252	Ava	278
3	Mason	246	Emma	228
4	Elijah	239	Amelia	195
5	William	228	Harper	187

Maine				
Rank	Male name	Number of males	Female name	Number of females
1	Oliver	86	Charlotte	89
2	Lincoln	66	Olivia	74
3	Liam	62	Emma	70
4	Owen	62	Harper	65
5	Wyatt	59	Amelia	56

Maryland				
Rank	Male name	Number of males	Female name	Number of females
1	Liam	341	Ava	341
2	Noah	297	Olivia	283
3	James	282	Emma	266
4	Logan	279	Sophia	258
5	Jacob	278	Charlotte	220

Massachusetts				
Rank	Male name	Number of males	Female name	Number of females
1	Benjamin	492	Emma	393
2	William	421	Olivia	379
3	Liam	373	Charlotte	347
4	Lucas	373	Sophia	330
5	Noah	365	Isabella	294

Michigan

Rank	Male name	Number of males	Female name	Number of females
1	Liam	505	Emma	531
2	Noah	476	Ava	526
3	Oliver	459	Olivia	505
4	Lucas	436	Charlotte	421
5	Mason	432	Amelia	409

Minnesota

Rank	Male name	Number of males	Female name	Number of females
1	Oliver	357	Olivia	310
2	William	343	Evelyn	307
3	Henry	337	Emma	296
4	Liam	299	Charlotte	259
5	Theodore	264	Nora	235

Mississippi				
Rank	Male name	Number of males	Female name	Number of females
1	William	180	Ava	211
2	John	179	Emma	151
3	James	166	Olivia	128
4	Mason	165	Paisley	105
5	Elijah	157	Amelia	97

Missouri				
Rank	Male name	Number of males	Female name	Number of females
1	William	345	Olivia	367
2	Liam	341	Ava	351
3	Oliver	318	Emma	341
4	Noah	315	Amelia	318
5	Elijah	301	Harper	296

Montana				
Rank	Male name	Number of males	Female name	Number of females
1	James	59	Olivia	59
2	William	57	Emma	53
3	Liam	53	Harper	45
4	Oliver	50	Ava	44
5	Wyatt	47	Charlotte	37

Nebraska				
Rank	Male name	Number of males	Female name	Number of females
1	Oliver	147	Emma	124
2	Liam	123	Olivia	115
3	William	118	Amelia	103
4	Henry	105	Charlotte	103
5	Noah	96	Evelyn	90

Nevada

Rank	Male name	Number of males	Female name	Number of females
1	Liam	196	Emma	187
2	Noah	167	Mia	181
3	Elijah	155	Isabella	170
4	Michael	145	Sophia	168
5	Sebastian	140	Olivia	163

New Hampshire

Rank	Male name	Number of males	Female name	Number of females
1	Logan	78	Charlotte	95
2	Henry	69	Evelyn	74
3	Mason	67	Emma	68
4	Owen	67	Olivia	67
5	Oliver	65	Amelia	58

New Jersey				
Rank	Male name	Number of males	Female name	Number of females
1	Liam	582	Emma	583
2	Noah	545	Olivia	561
3	Matthew	521	Isabella	535
4	Michael	496	Mia	456
5	Jacob	474	Sophia	440

New Mexico				
Rank	Male name	Number of males	Female name	Number of females
1	Noah	129	Mia	107
2	Santiago	96	Sophia	102
3	Elijah	94	Isabella	91
4	Liam	91	Olivia	88
5	Daniel	89	Ava	72

New York				
Rank	Male name	Number of males	Female name	Number of females
1	Liam	1,427	Olivia	1,227
2	Noah	1,238	Emma	1,204
3	Jacob	1,141	Sophia	1,007
4	Lucas	1,047	Mia	996
5	Joseph	1,014	Ava	987

North Carolina				
Rank	Male name	Number of males	Female name	Number of females
1	William	629	Ava	649
2	Noah	621	Emma	586
3	Liam	571	Olivia	583
4	James	537	Isabella	430
5	Mason	522	Charlotte	417

North Dakota				
Rank	Male name	Number of males	Female name	Number of females
1	Oliver	74	Emma	70
2	Henry	64	Harper	61
3	Liam	61	Olivia	53
4	Noah	51	Amelia	51
5	William	49	Ava	49

Ohio				
Rank	Male name	Number of males	Female name	Number of females
1	Liam	652	Emma	669
2	Carter	586	Ava	661
3	Noah	585	Olivia	621
4	William	556	Harper	559
5	Lucas	539	Charlotte	525

Oklahoma

Rank	Male name	Number of males	Female name	Number of females
1	William	199	Emma	234
2	Liam	196	Olivia	199
3	Noah	189	Harper	184
4	Elijah	183	Ava	177
5	James	181	Isabella	159

Oregon

Rank	Male name	Number of males	Female name	Number of females
1	Oliver	229	Emma	208
2	Liam	216	Olivia	207
3	Henry	193	Sophia	158
4	Benjamin	190	Charlotte	150
5	William	178	Evelyn	146

Pennsylvania

Rank	Male name	Number of males	Female name	Number of females
1	Liam	718	Emma	778
2	Noah	683	Olivia	666
3	Logan	670	Ava	620
4	Benjamin	632	Charlotte	506
5	Mason	616	Sophia	498

Rhode Island

Rank	Male name	Number of males	Female name	Number of females
1	Lucas	64	Charlotte	69
2	Liam	61	Emma	67
3	Noah	61	Olivia	63
4	Julian	59	Sophia	60
5	Mason	56	Isabella	51

South Carolina

Rank	Male name	Number of males	Female name	Number of females
1	William	324	Ava	289
2	Noah	285	Emma	255
3	Mason	267	Olivia	221
4	James	251	Charlotte	192
5	Liam	231	Harper	187

South Dakota

Rank	Male name	Number of males	Female name	Number of females
1	Oliver	67	Emma	53
2	Owen	62	Olivia	50
3	Lincoln	56	Harper	47
4	Liam	53	Evelyn	46
5	William	50	Nora	45

Tennessee				
Rank	Male name	Number of males	Female name	Number of females
1	William	526	Ava	435
2	Elijah	436	Olivia	394
3	James	401	Emma	376
4	Noah	367	Amelia	310
5	Mason	339	Harper	308

Texas				
Rank	Male name	Number of males	Female name	Number of females
1	Noah	1,942	Emma	2,302
2	Liam	1,830	Mia	1,882
3	Sebastian	1,585	Isabella	1,828
4	Mateo	1,511	Sophia	1,814
5	Elijah	1,469	Olivia	1,764

Utah				
Rank	Male name	Number of males	Female name	Number of females
1	Oliver	297	Olivia	245
2	Liam	265	Emma	233
3	William	247	Charlotte	211
4	James	244	Evelyn	191
5	Benjamin	205	Hazel	179

Vermont				
Rank	Male name	Number of males	Female name	Number of females
1	Wyatt	36	Evelyn	34
2	William	32	Olivia	29
3	Oliver	31	Charlotte	28
4	Liam	30	Emma	27
5	Noah	29	Harper	24

Virginia				
Rank	Male name	Number of males	Female name	Number of females
1	Liam	541	Olivia	474
2	William	525	Ava	458
3	Noah	497	Emma	437
4	James	468	Charlotte	418
5	Benjamin	367	Isabella	348

Washington				
Rank	Male name	Number of males	Female name	Number of females
1	Liam	421	Olivia	428
2	Oliver	410	Emma	421
3	Noah	352	Evelyn	336
4	William	347	Ava	309
5	Benjamin	341	Isabella	308

West Virginia				
Rank	Male name	Number of males	Female name	Number of females
1	Liam	133	Emma	111
2	Mason	98	Olivia	94
3	Elijah	96	Harper	88
4	Grayson	92	Paisley	79
5	Carter	90	Amelia	77

Wisconsin				
Rank	Male name	Number of males	Female name	Number of females
1	Henry	328	Emma	312
2	Oliver	322	Olivia	312
3	Liam	283	Evelyn	294
4	William	281	Charlotte	278
5	Logan	268	Ava	273

Wyoming				
Rank	Male name	Number of males	Female name	Number of females
1	Liam	30	Emma	35
2	Wyatt	30	Harper	24
3	Carter	28	Ava	23
4	James	27	Avery	21
5	Logan	27	Charlotte	21

Most Popular Names From 1914-2014				
	Males		Females	
Rank	Name	Number	Name	Number
1	James	4,866,619	Mary	3,611,970
2	John	4,739,937	Patricia	1,566,673
3	Robert	4,663,044	Jennifer	1,461,186
4	Michael	4,274,035	Elizabeth	1,460,714
5	William	3,749,398	Linda	1,447,270
6	David	3,532,745	Barbara	1,419,954
7	Richard	2,514,061	Susan	1,107,871
8	Joseph	2,429,076	Margaret	1,075,828
9	Charles	2,202,425	Jessica	1,038,248
10	Thomas	2,189,914	Sarah	1,009,728
11	Christopher	1,981,942	Dorothy	996,176
12	Daniel	1,833,861	Karen	982,864

13	Matthew	1,535,504	Nancy	980,659
14	Donald	1,392,452	Betty	978,903
15	Anthony	1,374,826	Lisa	963,461
16	Paul	1,338,796	Sandra	871,935
17	Mark	1,337,781	Helen	839,049
18	George	1,279,176	Ashley	831,126
19	Steven	1,269,104	Donna	827,839
20	Kenneth	1,250,728	Kimberly	825,188
21	Andrew	1,220,464	Carol	813,104
22	Edward	1,183,885	Michelle	802,726
23	Joshua	1,162,595	Emily	776,588
24	Brian	1,155,378	Amanda	769,412
25	Kevin	1,147,194	Melissa	746,598
26	Ronald	1,073,055	Deborah	738,182
27	Timothy	1,055,093	Laura	737,287
28	Jason	1,008,367	Stephanie	732,475
29	Jeffrey	968,779	Rebecca	727,122
30	Gary	897,536	Sharon	720,198
31	Ryan	891,166	Cynthia	703,977
32	Nicholas	866,148	Kathleen	700,446
33	Eric	861,720	Ruth	690,702
34	Jacob	848,038	Anna	688,230
35	Stephen	842,384	Shirley	680,162
36	Jonathan	803,785	Amy	673,299
37	Larry	801,570	Angela	653,815

38	Frank	792,425	Virginia	605,681
39	Scott	766,917	Brenda	605,336
40	Justin	758,002	Pamela	593,379
41	Brandon	734,956	Catherine	589,636
42	Raymond	730,505	Katherine	584,301
43	Gregory	702,296	Nicole	577,390
44	Samuel	673,653	Christine	571,921
45	Benjamin	660,859	Janet	550,377
46	Patrick	654,333	Debra	550,114
47	Jack	624,651	Samantha	549,656
48	Dennis	611,088	Carolyn	547,182
49	Jerry	604,399	Rachel	543,294
50	Alexander	596,167	Heather	523,369
51	Tyler	564,635	Maria	520,013
52	Henry	552,764	Diane	517,239
53	Douglas	552,541	Frances	507,194
54	Peter	549,126	Joyce	503,943
55	Aaron	542,328	Julie	503,658
56	Walter	539,969	Emma	482,694
57	Jose	535,132	Evelyn	477,717
58	Adam	524,872	Martha	477,345
59	Zachary	513,121	Joan	477,063
60	Harold	510,935	Kelly	468,441
61	Nathan	503,723	Christina	468,006
62	Kyle	468,806	Lauren	456,337

63	Carl	467,691	Judith	449,584
64	Arthur	459,623	Alice	446,529
65	Gerald	440,160	Victoria	446,019
66	Roger	434,033	Doris	441,420
67	Lawrence	432,407	Ann	441,101
68	Keith	430,907	Jean	440,900
69	Albert	426,595	Cheryl	438,916
70	Jeremy	425,094	Marie	438,758
71	Terry	420,348	Megan	433,186
72	Joe	415,584	Kathryn	423,415
73	Sean	409,292	Andrea	420,518
74	Willie	401,244	Jacqueline	415,334
75	Jesse	387,718	Gloria	407,880
76	Austin	382,419	Teresa	406,116
77	Christian	381,911	Janice	403,901
78	Ralph	380,721	Sara	402,166
79	Billy	380,571	Rose	393,573
80	Bruce	376,305	Hannah	393,208
81	Bryan	369,632	Julia	392,864
82	Roy	366,779	Theresa	384,281
83	Eugene	357,110	Judy	380,857
84	Ethan	355,803	Grace	378,602
85	Louis	351,563	Beverly	375,754
86	Wayne	346,862	Denise	370,776
87	Jordan	345,140	Marilyn	367,206

88	Harry	342,952	Mildred	366,723
89	Russell	336,600	Amber	365,710
90	Alan	335,720	Danielle	362,010
91	Juan	328,239	Brittany	355,762
92	Philip	325,446	Olivia	352,263
93	Randy	325,386	Diana	351,810
94	Dylan	321,319	Jane	349,812
95	Howard	316,046	Lori	340,265
96	Vincent	315,590	Madison	336,143
97	Bobby	311,783	Tiffany	333,625
98	Johnny	305,004	Kathy	332,976
99	Phillip	300,279	Tammy	331,500
100	Shawn	298,043	Crystal	326,726

First Trimester

During the first trimester, just go with the flow. Your baby does not care about your schedule.

Get Your Health in Order

The first few weeks of fetal development are crucial; eat well and healthy. "By the time you miss one period, 80 percent of organ development has happened. The heart, face, limbs -- anything likely to have a defect has formed," says Robert Greene, PhD, director of the Birth Defects Center at the University of Louisville.

Do not smoke, drink, or take a multivitamin with folic acid before trying to get pregnant. If you were unhealthy before you knew about the baby, do not dwell on it. Instead, focus on what you can do now to have a healthy newborn.

Call Your OB/GYN

It is important to see your doctor in the first trimester, often around eight weeks. The doctor will listen for a robust heartbeat (this will also confirm the number of fetuses, depending upon the number of heartbeats).

This is an important time for you to ask any questions you may have, such as your due date.

Sleep and Eat

The most common symptom of early pregnancy is exhaustion. It is okay to sleep whenever you need it, especially since once the baby is born, you may not get the chance. As mentioned earlier, cravings will be normal, usually in response to a nutritional deficiency. Morning sickness can occur. Neither is a cause for concern, unless you are unable to keep anything down, or you crave nonfood items such as dirt or soap. In either case, to be on the safe side, call your doctor right away for medical intervention.

Childcare

If you plan to return to work after having the baby, you need to be thinking about childcare way before the delivery date. Many daycare centers will have no idea when they will have an opening. Get your name on a list.

Second Trimester

You Must Tell Your Boss

For many women, this can be a nerve-racking experience, but you need to do it. It is understandable that most women wait to tell their boss until they are in their second trimester, when the risk of miscarriage declines.

Buy Maternity Clothes

Most women do not need maternity clothes until their second trimester. Nonetheless, be prepared – you will need them.

Start a Registry for Your Baby

Tori Binau, senior vice president of marketing at Babies "R" Us, says most women register in their sixth month, a timeframe she sees as ideal. "When we see moms well into their third trimester, registering doesn't look as fun as it should be," she says. You need to give yourself time to add to, change, and tweak your registry.

Get Your Household Organized

Baby will be demanding the majority of your attention when you get home. Organize now to make it easier after giving birth. Set up files for bill paying, recipes, or whatever else could use organization. Do your Spring-cleaning now. After all, once the baby is born, you most likely will not be organized for a very long time.

Third Trimester

Install the Car Seat
This is one of the most important things you will need to do.

According to the National Highway Traffic Safety Administration, more than 80 % of car safety seats are not installed correctly. Have yours inspected before it is time for baby to ride home. To locate a child seat fitting station, call 1-866-SEAT-CHECK or go to seatcheck.org. Give yourself a few weeks, because you might need to make an appointment.

Get Serious About a Baby Name
If you have not decided on a name by now, the middle of the third trimester is the best time to sit down and hash it out. Any earlier and you might suffer weeks of baby-name strife. Any later, and you and your partner might be negotiating a name in the recovery room.

When to Stop Working
Most women can safely work to the end of their pregnancy, but check with your doctor first. If time is not a factor for you, it's nice to have a week or so before giving birth to pull everything together.

Find Time for Each Other

For the first few months (or more) after the baby is born, you and your partner will not have a lot of alone time. Schedule as many "date nights" as you can before your little bundle of joy arrives.

Give Birth

The time is here. Just remember there are a few thinks you should not say during labor and delivery like "Is It Ok If I Quickly Check The Score?" or "OMG, Gross..." or "I'm Exhausted." I'm pretty sure you are have as exhausted as the one having the baby. Now enjoy the happiest day of your life!

Morning Sickness

According to Wikipedia, morning sickness affects more than half of all pregnant women. In fact, nausea and vomiting are often the first signs of pregnancy and usually begin six weeks after conception. The symptoms are present in the early morning hours and will reduce as the day progresses. Still, morning sickness is somewhat of a misnomer, as it can occur at any time of the day. For most women it usually stops around the 12th week of pregnancy.

That said, there are some women who experience a very severe form of morning sickness known as hyperemesis gravidarum. As excessive vomiting can cause dehydration, weight loss, alkalosis (the opposite of acidosis), and hypokalemia (low potassium levels), you should call you doctor if this occurs. The good news is it only occurs in about 1% of all pregnancies.

Some Causes of Morning Sickness

1. During the first trimester, there can be an increase in salivation. It is often bitter tasting. While sleeping, the saliva is ingested into the stomach, thus upsetting it enough to cause the morning nausea.
2. The placenta can drain energy from the mother, creating low blood sugar or "hypoglycemia". Please note that studies have not confirmed this except in expectant mothers with Type 1 diabetes.
3. GERD, or gastro esophageal reflux disease, is excessive stomach acid that passes up from the stomach and into the esophagus, often causing nausea. During pregnancy, an increase in the steroid hormone progesterone relaxes the muscles in the uterus (a natural occurrence that prevents early childbirth); it also may relax the stomach and intestines, leading to excess stomach acids.
4. Sensitivity to odors during a pregnancy can over-stimulate normal nausea triggers.
5. During a pregnancy, an increased level of bilirubin (a brownish yellow substance found in bile) due to increased liver enzymes, can also cause nausea.

Morning Sickness as a Defense Mechanism

As unpleasant as it is, morning sickness is actually an evolved trait that protects the fetus against toxins. A mom-to-be may experience nausea when exposed to the smell or taste of foods that are likely to contain toxins injurious to the fetus.

If a pregnant woman does not experience morning sickness, she is at a higher risk to miscarry. This may be because such women are more likely to ingest substances that are harmful to the fetus.

Morning sickness may also protect the mother. A pregnant woman's immune system is suppressed during pregnancy. It is presumed that this is to reduce the chances of rejecting tissues of her own offspring. The risk of animal products that contain parasites and harmful bacteria can be especially dangerous to pregnant women. Perhaps as a defense mechanism against parasites and harmful bacteria, morning sickness is often triggered by the smell of animal products, including meat and fish. Therefore, prescribing anti-nausea medication to the mom-to-be may have the undesired side effect of causing birth defects or miscarriages by encouraging harmful dietary choices.

Packing for the Hospital

The Baby Center website suggests you divide items into two bags -- one for items you will need during labor, and one for the items you will use after the baby is born.

Bring your photo ID. In addition, you will need your insurance card. If you have questions, bring your notes. Pack instructions from your doctor or lactation counselor.

Pack toothpaste and a toothbrush. Bring lotions, lip balm, or any other item that will help keep you comfortable. You may need to pack hair clips or holders to keep your hair off your face. Pack a hairbrush. You may choose to bring your favorite shampoo, conditioner, or soap. You deserve to be pampered.

Don't forget your glasses or contacts, and be sure to bring all your medications.

Pack a comfortable robe and slippers, a nightgown (Baby Center suggests bringing two nightgowns), and loose-fitting clothes with non-binding waistbands (Southeast Georgia Health System suggests an outfit you would have worn in your fifth month of pregnancy). Bring a pair of thick socks to wear during labor. You might want to pack flip-flops. If you are going to breastfeed, don't forget a nursing bra. Do not forget an outfit for the baby, and blankets for the trip home. You may need a newborn diaper. Check with your hospital to see if they provide them – most do.

Absolutely do not forget the memory-catchers. You will want a video camera or smart phone with video capability so the proud spouse and others can take pictures. Also, be sure to pack a baby book for putting baby's hand and footprints.

You might want to bring makeup. It will make you feel better before the adoring guests arrive.

How to Prepare for Baby

Car seat

Hospitals will not let new parents take their child home without a properly installed car seat.

Diaper Care Items

It is essential to have diaper care products in the house before your due date, as it will be one less thing to worry about when your baby arrives home. It is advised that you purchase diapers and wipes in large quantities, as this will save you both time and money. Soft washcloths and diaper cream will also be needed. Most newborns have sensitive skin and frequently develop diaper rash. If you have decided on using cloth diapers, you will need to have diaper detergent and a diaper bag on hand.

Essential Care Products

For bathing your newborn, you will need baby shampoo and soft washcloths and baby towels. Consider using a small baby bathtub combined with a mesh bath lounger to make bathing your newborn child easier. You will also need a small comb or soft-bristled baby brush to brush the newborn's hair. Some parents prefer to use baby bubble bath to soothe the infant during its bath. A baby's skin is very delicate and using lotion will help to prevent it from becoming dry. Always keep on hand a thermometer (ear or rectal will be the most accurate), and a nasal aspirator and medicine dropper in case the baby becomes ill. Use nail clippers designed for a baby to prevent him/her from scratching their face.

Feeding Items

Expectant parents should decide how they plan to feed the newborn and shop for the appropriate items. Have those items in the home before going to the hospital to deliver. You want to make sure that feeding time goes smoothly when you get home.

If you have chosen to breastfeed, purchase breast pads and Lansinoh cream to increase comfort during the early weeks of nursing. You will also need a breast pump, a breast milk storage bag and bottles, particularly if you are still breastfeeding after returning to work. If you have chosen to bottle-feed your baby, you should buy a few cans of formula and plenty of bottles. Some mothers prefer to stock up on baby food before the baby is born to avoid last minute shopping. Baby dishes can be purchased early and kept in a cupboard. However you decide to feed your baby, you will need bibs and burp cloths.

Baby Furniture

It is very important that the expectant parents have all the necessary furniture set up before bringing their newborn home. This includes such items as a crib, playpen, stroller, and, of course, a car seat. You may consider purchasing an infant swing to help soothe the fussy baby. You will probably want a changing table, as it can be helpful to raise the infant up to a high level during diaper changes. When setting up the infant's crib, parents should use the appropriate bedding--no bumpers, pillows or heavy bedding should be used, only soft sheets and light blankets.

Baby Clothing

You want to have plenty of items on hand for baby to wear, so stocking up is important. You will find that your newborn can soil clothing often throughout the day. It would be best if you can have three to four outfit choices for each day of the week, along with two or three changes of clothing for naps and bedtime. Consider using onesies, sleepers, pants, shirts, socks, hats, and scratch mitts.

Baby Toys

Toys can be useful in calming your newborn, so you might want to have them available as soon as he or she comes home. Soft, plush toys provide a comfort and sensory experience for young babies. Read large and brightly colored board books to newborns to encourage language and visual development. Most infants like small, noisy items that are easy to grasp. Place mirrors or mobiles above the crib and changing station. This will entertain your baby during diaper changing or alone times.

What Should a New Mom Do When She Gets Home?

A new mom should take the first two weeks to be with her baby. Let others do everything else that needs to be done. Mom needs time to heal.

It is okay if the baby sleeps in the bed with you, or in the crib. The most important thing is that both mom and baby are getting sleep.

If the baby is going to sleep alone, remove all toys from the crib before placing your baby in it. Use a light blanket. Long-sleeved pajamas will help to keep baby warm at night. You may think about using crib bumpers to prevent the baby from hitting his/her head on the sides of the crib.

Avoid daily baths for the first few weeks. They are not necessary and may dry out the baby's skin. Instead, use baby wipes or washcloths to clean soiled areas. When it is time for a bath, a sponge bath will suffice. Fill a baby tub with lukewarm water and use a soap developed for babies. Make sure you have a diaper and change of clothes ready to dress the baby immediately so he/she doesn't get cold after the bath.

Germ Free
A new mom has to be germ conscious.
As soon as you bring your baby home, family and friends will naturally be anxious to see the newborn. Before placing your baby in their arms, make sure your guests wash their hands first. Your baby's immune system is very weak, so it will be difficult for him or her to fight off germs. Be sure and place hand sanitizer around your house for those impromptu moments.

Schedule an Appointment
One of the first things you should do after bringing the baby home is to schedule the first doctor appointment; otherwise, you will get lost in the whirlwind of diaper changing and feedings. Find out what shots your baby will need. The sooner you start this process the better. Remember, your newborn is fending off germs and will need the extra protection from various diseases.

Five Things Grandparents Can Do to Help

If you and your partner are lucky enough to have your parents around, they can be a big help when taking care of your baby. Grandparents tend to spoil the grandchild, and why not? They already did the hard work when they raised their own kids; now it's their time to play the hero, the saint. After all they probably endured when you were growing up, they deserve it.

That said, a good grandparent knows that in the story of their grandchildren's lives, they are an important supporting character, *not* the star. A good grandparent will always respect what the new parents have to say. They will respect the decisions they make in raising their own children. And, yes, we already know they didn't do it that way "in your day".

Here are five things grandparents can do to help the new parents:

1. Grandparents can make sure the new parents get the bonding time they will need when baby first comes home. If the new parents are holding the baby when the grandparents come over, let them. When they are ready to let Grandma or Grandpa hold the little one for extended periods, they'll let you know, but don't take away their bonding time, unless they willingly allow it. The desire to want to hold the baby is a tough thing for grandma and grandpa to fight. After all, it brings back those fondest of memories.

2. Grandma and Grandpa can help the new mom around the house by doing dishes, preparing meals, taking out trash, and doing the shopping, especially when the spouse is working.

3. Be understanding when the new mom snaps back at you. Remember, she just gave birth. Grandma will definitely understand; Grandpa, on the other hand, may flee the scene and go on an unplanned errand.

4. Always be encouraging. Remember how tough it was for you when you had your first child.

5. Never give unsolicited advice.

Surviving the First Six Weeks

Listen to Your Instincts
Do not depend on the internet. If you know your baby is hungry, feed him.

Listen and Watch for Your Baby's Cues
Newborns communicate only through body language and crying. However, within weeks they will rapidly begin to develop behavioral patterns, such as different tones of crying. They are clearly trying to tell you something. Maybe they are hungry, or perhaps the diaper needs changing. Listen for the difference. Some babies may give you cues for hunger way before crying. This can include such things as finger sucking and reaching with arms and legs. Once you figure out the cues, it is to your advantage to act promptly. Otherwise, the shrieking that will follow may leave your ears ringing. You may notice the baby pulling at his/her ears, yawning and/or quick, jerky movements. Try to decipher what it is your baby is trying to tell you. The quicker you learn, the easier it will be to stop the uncontrollable crying.

Nursing vs. Formula Feeding

Nursing is hard - extremely hard—and will take a fair amount of time, discomfort, and practice for both you and your baby to get the hang of it. Do not be afraid to ask for help from a friend, family member or even a lactation consultant.

You may find that breastfeeding is not for you. You or your baby may have a medical condition that prevents you from nursing. Whatever the reason, it should never be considered a failure if you don't breastfeed.

Regardless of what you do, the most important thing is to make sure your baby will grow up beautiful, wonderful, smart, and articulate. You have to do what is best for you and your child. Do not let anyone make you feel inadequate, regardless of your decision.

Don't Try to be the Perfect Mom

Is anyone truly the perfect mom? All that is expected of you is that you try your best. Parenting is filled with both triumphs and failures. You should never be hard on yourself or get discouraged. There is always an answer, so find it. Practice makes perfect.

Oftentimes, the hardest thing to do is also the wisest thing. If Grandma, Grandpa, Brother, or Sister wants to bring over dinner, let them. If someone wants to come over while you take a nap and shower, go for it. Learn the importance of graciously accept all the help you can get. Don't be afraid to ask for help.

Make Time for Your Partner

We talked about this earlier - do not lose sight of your relationship with your partner. Between the exhaustion from the sleepless nights, the demanding feeding schedule and your normal household or work activities, it will be hard to carve out quality time, but it is very important. Remember, your relationship is what created that little one in the first place, so find the time to say "I Love You". It is okay to make the baby the center of your attention, as long as not all of it is directed to the child.

Take Time for Yourself

Make time for yourself, every day. Go for a fifteen-minute walk. Make a quick trip to the corner market. Take a shower, put on clean clothes, and eat at least two full meals a day. Getting away for just a little bit will help you rejuvenate.

You just gave birth. Remember, in order to take care of your baby, you need to take care of yourself.

How to Hold a Newborn Baby

Be calm and confident before picking up the baby. Babies can often sense if you are uncomfortable or upset. Relax. Though it is important to be as careful as possible, babies are not as fragile as you think.

Support the baby's head with one arm and support its bottom with the other. A newborn baby's head is by far the heaviest part of his or her body, and a baby's head and neck needs careful support. Usually you will hold the head gently with one hand. Use your right arm to scoop up the baby's bottom. Do this while supporting the head with your other hand.

Make chest-to-chest contact. Bring the baby close to your chest, so that he or she can rest his or her head against your chest. Babies are instinctively comforted by hearing your heartbeat. Your right hand and arm should be supporting most of the baby's body weight, while your left hand supports and protects the head and neck. Just make sure that your baby's head is facing to one side so that he or she can always breathe.

Enjoy bonding with the baby. Holding a baby can be incredibly soothing for both of you. This is a great time to sing to the baby, read to the baby, and entertain the baby until it is time for the next feeding, diaper change, or nap. You will need to switch hands from time to time. When you do this, remember to always keep one hand under the baby's head.

Listen to your baby. Each baby has its own preferences for how he or she wants to be held. If your baby is crying or being fussy, try switching positions.

What to Expect After Giving Birth

If you have a natural childbirth, while holding the baby you might have a doctor halfway up your body stitching you, or a nurse pumping your stomach to help you deliver the placenta. You will most likely be in pain and overwhelmed with exhaustion.

Your first trip to the bathroom after you deliver will be an experience you probably won't forget. Let someone help you. You do not want to risk passing out alone.

Most moms report that breastfeeding hurts in the beginning... sometimes a lot. A Lactation Consultant is your best bet.

During the first few days of postpartum, you will most likely cry ... a lot. After all, your hormones are a wreck. Your partner will most likely not be your favorite person. After all, HE CAUSED THIS!

Seriously, though, if you are extremely irritable and cannot overcome depression, seek professional help.

Contrary to what you may have been told, be prepared … babies do not sleep all the time.

Now that you are prepared, sit back and enjoy the miracle that is about to change your life forever!